# Alaska

BY MARI KESSELRING

**The Child's World**

Published by The Child's World®
1980 Lookout Drive • Mankato, MN  56003-1705
800-599-READ • www.childsworld.com

ACKNOWLEDGMENTS
The Child's World®: Mary Berendes, Publishing Director
The Design Lab: Design and production
Red Line Editorial: Editorial direction

PHOTO CREDITS: Iztok Noc/iStockphoto, cover, 1, 3; Matt Kania/Map
Hero, Inc., 4, 5; iStockphoto, 7, 10; Paul Tessier/iStockphoto, 9; Maurice
van der Velden/iStockphoto, 11; Tom Tietz/iStockphoto, 13; North Wind
Picture Archives/Photolibrary, 15; Gus Ruelas/AP Images, 17; Matt Cooper/
Shutterstock Images, 19; Oksana Perkins/iStockphoto, 21; One Mile Up, 22;
Quarter-dollar coin image from the United States Mint, 22

LIBRARY OF CONGRESS CATALOGING-IN-PUBLICATION DATA
Kesselring, Mari.
 Alaska / by Mari Kesselring.
   p. cm.
 Includes bibliographical references and index.
 ISBN 978-1-60253-446-9 (library bound : alk. paper)
 1. Alaska—Juvenile literature.  I. Title.

F904.3.K47 2010
979.8—dc22

2010016163

Printed in the United States of America in Mankato, Minnesota.
July 2010
F11538

On the cover:
Alaska is well
known for dog
sledding.

CONTENTS

# Geography

Let's explore Alaska! Alaska is the northern-most state. It is also the largest state. It does not touch any other state. Alaska shares its eastern border with Canada. Three of its sides are surrounded by water.

Alaska is only about 50 miles (80 km) away from Russia.

Arctic Ocean

RUSSIA

• Barrow

Prudhoe
Bay

**ALASKA**

Nome

Fairbanks

CANADA

Mount
McKinley ▲

Alaska
Range

NORTH
WEST          EAST
SOUTH

Bering
Sea

Anchorage •          • Valdez

Kenai •

• Skagway

**Juneau**

Sitka •

Unalaska •

Ketchikan •

Pacific Ocean

# Cities

Juneau is the capital of Alaska. Juneau was originally a **popular** city because gold was found there. Today, many people visit the city. Anchorage is the biggest city in Alaska. Nome and Fairbanks are other well-known cities.

Juneau is home to about 31,000 people. ▶

# Land

Alaska has a lot of flat **tundra**. It also has high mountains. Mount McKinley in Alaska is the highest mountain in North America. It is part of a group of mountains called the Alaska Range. These mountains separate the coast from the tundra.

Parts of Mount McKinley are covered in snow even during summer. ▶

Mount McKinley
is 20,320 feet
(6,194 m) high.

# Plants and Animals

Pine trees grow in many parts of Alaska. These trees stay green all year. Alaska's state flower is the forget-me-not. The state bird is the willow ptarmigan. It has brown and white feathers during the warm part of the year. It turns completely white during winter. This helps the bird hide in the snow.

The forget-me-not grows best in shade. ▶

# People and Work

Almost 700,000 people live in Alaska. It is home to many people who work in the **military**. Alaska has a lot of oil. Many people work in jobs with oil. Other people fish or help those who travel to the state.

Only Wyoming, North Dakota, and Vermont have fewer people than Alaska.

Fishermen on a fishing boat in Alaska haul up their catch. ▶

# History

People first came to Alaska thousands of years ago. The United States bought Alaska from Russia in 1867. Alaska became the forty-ninth state on January 3, 1959.

The Inuit are **native** people in Alaska. ▶

# Ways of Life

Sports such as skiing, hockey, and dog sledding are very popular in Alaska. One well-known event is the Iditarod Trail Sled Dog Race. Around 100 people race in the event each year. Each person has about 12 to 16 dogs that help him or her. The race takes about 10 to 17 days to finish.

A man and his dogs race in the Iditarod Trail Sled Dog Race. ▶

# Famous People

Actress Irene Bedard was born in Alaska. She was the voice of Pocahontas in Disney's *Pocahontas*. Country singer Jewel grew up in Alaska. She has written many popular songs. Former Alaska governor Sarah Palin also grew up in the state.

Jewel writes songs, sings, and plays guitar. ▶

# Famous Places

Alaska has many national parks. They are great places for outdoor activities such as camping, fishing, and **hiking**. Alaska also has many **museums**. The state has several events that focus on the native people's **cultures**.

Alaska is home to many animals, including brown bears. ▶

# State Symbols

### Seal

Alaska's state seal shows the natural beauty of the state. It also shows how important fishing and mining are. Go to childsworld.com/links for a link to Alaska's state Web site, where you can get a firsthand look at the state seal.

### Flag

The dark blue background on the state flag is meant to remind people of the Alaskan sky. The seven gold stars form the Big Dipper. These stars can be seen easily in Alaska.

### Quarter

The Alaska state quarter shows a grizzly bear. It stands for Alaska's many animals. The quarter came out in 2008.

# Glossary

**cultures** (KUL-churz): Cultures refer to the art and manners of groups of people. The cultures of Alaska's native people can be seen throughout the state.

**hiking** (HYK-ing): Hiking is taking a walk in a natural area, such as a hill or a mountain. Many people in Alaska enjoy hiking.

**military** (MIL-uh-tayr-ee): The military is the armed forces of a country. Many people in Alaska are in the military.

**museums** (myoo-ZEE-umz): Museums are places where people go to see art, history, or science displays. People in Alaska visit museums.

**native** (NAY-tiv): Native means from a certain area. Native Alaskans are proud of their culture and history.

**popular** (POP-yuh-lur): To be popular is to be enjoyed by many people. Dog sledding is popular in Alaska.

**seal** (SEEL): A seal is a symbol a state uses for government business. The Alaska state seal shows the nature in the state.

**symbols** (SIM-bulz): Symbols are pictures or things that stand for something else. The flag and seal are Alaska's symbols.

**tundra** (TUN-druh): A tundra is a very cold area with no trees. Tundra is common in Alaska.

# Further Information

## Books

Crane, Carol. *L is for Last Frontier: An Alaska Alphabet*. Chelsea, MI: Sleeping Bear Press, 2002.

Gill, Shelley. *Alaska*. Watertown, MA: Charlesbridge Publishing, 2007.

Miller, Debbie S. *Big Alaska: Journey Across America's Most Amazing State*. New York: Walker, 2006.

## Web Sites

Visit our Web site for links about Alaska: *childsworld.com/links*

Note to Parents, Teachers, and Librarians: We routinely verify our Web links to make sure they are safe and active sites. So encourage your readers to check them out!

# Index